A book to mark the 750th anniversary of the sealing of MAGNA CARTA and the 700th anniversary of the parliament of SIMON DE MONTFORT

The Charter of Liberties which we know as Magna Carta, sealed by King John 750 years ago, was not only of great significance in its own day but has also become, in the form in which it was issued by King Henry III in 1225, even more influential and important in later centuries. This grant of privileges in a land at that time still ruled by a feudal aristocracy guaranteed the liberties of the king's free subjects and restricted the powers of the king within certain well defined limits. Because of its application to conditions undreamed of by its authors and to the constitutions of countries then undiscovered, Magna Carta has become the most important single document in the development of constitutional and legal freedom not only in Britain but also in the United States of America and in many countries of the Commonwealth. Within recent years it has provided an example which has been followed in the Universal Declaration of Human Rights and the European Convention for the Protection of Human Rights and Fundamental Freedoms. The celebrations of Magna Carta are linked in Britain and abroad with the commemoration of Simon de Montfort's parliament held 700 years ago.

MAGNA CARTA

and its influence in the world today

BY SIR IVOR JENNINGS

KBE, QC, LittD, LLD

CONTENTS

PLATES

ACKNOWLEDGMENTS

Arbitrary Parliaments 1683: viii(*b*); AUSTRALIAN GOVERNMENT: xii(*b*), xii(*c*); BRITISH MUSEUM: Inside front cover, iii, iv, vi, vii(*a*), viii(*a*), x(*b*); CANADIAN GOVERNMENT: xii(*a*); CENTRAL PRESS PHOTOS: x(*d*); CROWN COPYRIGHT: i(*a*), x(*a*); GIRAUDON, PARIS: ii(*a*); HOUSE OF LORDS RECORDS OFFICE: ix; JELLICOE AND COLERIDGE: xvi(*b*); A. J. KERSTING: i(*c*), outside back cover; MANSELL COLLECTION: i(*b*); SYDNEY NEWBERRY: xvi(*a*); NEW ZEALAND GOVERNMENT: xiii(*a*), xiii(*b*); P. A. REUTERS: v; PUBLIC RECORDS OFFICE: ii(*b*); RADIO TIMES HULTON PICTURE LIBRARY: vii(*b*), outside back cover; *The Times*: xiv, xv; THOMSON NEWSPAPERS: xi; TRANSPORT HOUSE: x(*c*).

Message from Earl Warren
Chief Justice of the Supreme Court of the
United States of America

The Magna Carta, whose 750th anniversary we celebrate this year, is one of the greatest secular documents ever written. It symbolizes the basic elements of free government and notably the principle that all persons—powerful and lowly alike—stand as equals before the law. Thus came the doctrine that the law is above both the governor and the governed.

The significance of the Magna Carta transcends the historical confines of concessions wrung from an oppressive monarch by the feudal barons at Runnymede, for it has proved to be the germination of an ever-growing greatness. It marks the transition from concepts rooted in custom or tradition to statutes, constitutions, parliaments, and congresses.

Our Founding Fathers in America regarded its principles as their birthright. Our devotion to its tenets is no less today. Its vibrant words, such as 'We will sell to no man, we will not deny or delay to any man either justice or right', span the ages. It is the very essence of the Rule of Law as distinguished from the rule of men, even as law is the essence of freedom itself. For, as Sir Ivor Jennings has noted in his scholarly comments on the Great Charter which follow, 'Without law there is no liberty'.

THE AUTHOR

Sir Ivor Jennings, KBE, QC, LittD, LLD, is Master of Trinity Hall and Downing Professor of the Laws of England in the University of Cambridge. He is also a Bencher of the Honourable Society of Gray's Inn. He was called to the Bar in 1928 and appointed King's Counsel in 1949. He has been constitutional adviser to a number of governments, was knighted in 1948 on the advice of the Prime Minister of Ceylon, received the KBE in 1955 on the advice of the Prime Minister of Pakistan, and was invested with the Order of the Right Hand of Gurkha by the King of Nepal in 1959. He was Vice-Chancellor of the University of Ceylon from 1942 to 1955 and Vice-Chancellor of the University of Cambridge from 1961 to 1963. He has lectured at universities in Canada, Australia, New Zealand, India, Pakistan, Ceylon, Ghana and the United States of America. He is an honorary doctor of the Universities of Belfast, Bristol, Ceylon, Hong Kong, Leeds, Paris and Southampton. His books include *The British Constitution, Cabinet Government, Parliament, Party Politics* and *The Law and the Constitution.* His most recent work, most of which is as yet unpublished, has been on the Liberties of England.

I What is Magna Carta?

THE DOCUMENT USUALLY KNOWN AS MAGNA CARTA is a royal charter under the seal of King John granted 'in the meadow called Runnymede between Windsor and Staines' on 15 June 1215. In form, it is much like any other medieval charter. It is in Latin, is engrossed on parchment, and is authenticated by the King's seal. It is frequently said that King John 'signed' the charter. This is, however, a misunderstanding of the phrase *data per manum nostram* (given by our hand). Royal charters were not signed but sealed, and none of the four surviving copies contains a signature. One of the two copies in the British Museum looks like the original, because it was hurriedly written and contains emendations at the foot which were incorporated in the text in the other three copies, all of which were obviously written more at leisure.

King John's Charter has, nevertheless, unusual characteristics which justify the term 'Great Charter'. Though there were many charters granting liberties to monasteries, barons and boroughs, this one grants liberties 'to all the free men of our kingdom'. For that reason many copies were sealed and were sent to the cathedrals and to other places for safe deposit. Two of the four copies still surviving, those at Lincoln and Salisbury, are probably the only survivors of copies sent to all the cathedrals. The 'original' in the British Museum came from Dover Castle and was probably sent to the barons of the Cinque Ports, the five ancient ports on the south coast through which communications with the continent of Europe were maintained. Also, the 'liberties' granted were unusually wide and covered a large section of the medieval laws of England. The implications of the grant are even more important because the charter bore witness to the rule of feudal law that a king, as well as other men, was bound by the law. This concept, that all power came from the law and that no man, be he king or minister or private person, is above the law, is commonly called the Rule of Law or government according to law.

On the other hand, the document which was originally called Magna Carta was not King John's Charter of 1215 but King Henry's Charter of 1225. King John sought to repudiate his Charter almost as soon as it was sealed, and he appealed to the Pope, Innocent III, who on 24 August 1215 issued a bull annulling the Charter. It is unnecessary to ask whether this action had any legal validity, for King John died a year later and the barons who had the infant king, Henry III, in their custody, decided to issue a revised version of the Charter of 1215 in the name of the new king. This was done hurriedly and certain matters were left out with a promise that they would be considered. They were considered, and in 1217 two charters, the Charter of Liberties and the Charter of the Forest, based on the Charters of 1215 and 1216, were issued in the name of King Henry III. Soon after that king came of age, for some purposes he sought a grant of taxation; and in consideration of a grant of a fifteenth on movables he was induced to reissue the two Charters, with slight amendments, in 1225.

In 1237, Henry III issued another Charter confirming the two Charters of 1225, which were then referred to as 'Magna Carta' and 'Carta de Foresta' as if those terms were already in common use. The full title, *Magna Carta de Libertatibus Angliae*, or the Great Charter of the Liberties of England, was not used until 1297. As part of the settlement of a dispute between Edward I and the landowners in that year, it was agreed that the king should confirm the Charters. A writ was issued for the production of a copy of Magna Carta. This Magna Carta was the Charter of 1225. The return to the writ begins, in Latin, 'We have inspected the Great Charter of the said Henry, formerly King, our father, concerning the liberties of England, in these words . . .'. It then sets out the text of King Henry's Great Charter of 1225.

This *inspeximus*, as it was called, was enrolled on the Statute Roll and became, for lawyers, the authoritative text. Copies are to be found in the manuscript collections of statutes which barristers used to quote in the courts in Westminster Hall. When the ancient statutes were printed late in the fifteenth century the text used was that of 1297. Some printers, notably Tottel in the sixteenth century, divided the Charter into 'chapters' and provided an English translation. Tottel's version was apparently used by the great jurist, Sir Edward Coke, who was dismissed from the office of Chief Justice of the King's Bench by King James I. His *Institutes of the Laws of England* in four volumes, the last three of which were published in

1642 by order of the Long Parliament, has been the standard work on the laws of England for more than three centuries. Volume II is devoted to some ancient statutes. The first of these is Magna Carta, which is described as 'issued in the ninth year of Henry III', i.e. 1225; but the text is taken from the *inspeximus* of 1297 and is in the form printed by Tottel.

It may be assumed that all references to Magna Carta in the courts and the law books, until very recent times, derive from Coke's *Institutes*. The famous chapter which begins, in the English version, 'No free man shall be taken or imprisoned . . .', and ends 'We will sell to no man, we will not deny or defer [delay] to any man either justice or right', is referred to as Cap. 29. Indeed, it ought always so to be quoted, for it is this Cap. 29 which is the law of England and of many other countries. It is, however, almost exactly the same as the provisions of King John's Charter of 1215 which are usually printed as Caps. 39 and 40, and sometimes those provisions are quoted in error.

The Magna Carta of 1225 was confirmed at least fifty-five times, and by all the kings from Henry III to Henry V. The last known confirmation was in 1416, but there may have been later confirmations. The practice was for the Commons to petition that the Charters be kept in all points, the king assenting in parliament; and some of the records of parliaments have been lost. There are references to Magna Carta in statutes of 1429 and 1442; and a statute of 1472 refers to 'the laudable statute of Magna Carta'. It does not appear in the statutes of the Tudors, but provisions from it are recited in the Petition of Right, 1628, and the Act for the abolition of the Court of Star Chamber, 1641. The whole of Magna Carta remained on the statute book until the nineteenth century. The authoritative text, for legal purposes, is that published as 25 Edward I (i.e. the *inspeximus* of 1297) in the first volume of *Statutes of the Realm* (1820). Later in the nineteenth century obsolete provisions were repealed by Statute Law Revision Acts; but what is left, including the famous Cap. 29, is in the latest edition of *Statutes Revised* (1950) at page 31 of Volume I, where it appears as 25 Edward I.

Why, then, is King John's Charter of 1215 called Magna Carta? There are two explanations. The first is that most of the provisions of the Magna Carta of 1225 derive, with or without amendment, from

King John's Charter. That Charter is not the source of the liberties of England, and indeed there were earlier charters—one of which, that issued by King Henry I in 1100, supplied the precedent for the Charter of 1215—but it was the first to set out the royal obligations in considerable detail. Much of the importance of Magna Carta, both to contemporaries and to later generations, lay in that detail, which passed through the Charters of 1216 and 1217 to its final form in 1225.

The second explanation is that, until Sir William Blackstone published his book *The Great Charter* in 1759, there was great confusion, due to the thirteenth-century chroniclers. They thought that the Charters of 1215 and 1225 were identical. The text in use, even as late as the great debate on *Darnel's Case* in 1628, was that of 1297. None of the great lawyers who took part in that debate had seen the Charter of 1215, though shortly afterwards Sir Robert Cotton acquired the two copies which are now in the British Museum. Though John Selden pointed out that the text given by the chronicler Matthew Paris contained two provisions which were not in the printed version of Magna Carta, he like others assumed that the Magna Carta in force had first been 'enacted' by King John at Runnymede.

When Blackstone published the texts of all four Charters—those of 1215, 1216, 1217 and 1225—he gave the name Magna Carta to them all, and this tradition has been continued by the historians. It is not an inconvenient tradition, for there is a very large common element; and it is entirely proper to celebrate the 750th anniversary of Magna Carta in 1965. On the other hand, the Magna Carta which has been and still is part of the law of England, and the laws of many other countries to which the law of England has been exported, is the Charter of 1225, and references to Magna Carta in this book are, unless the context otherwise indicates, references to the 'statute' which may be described as 9 Henry III (1225) or 25 Edward I (1297).

II The Liberties of England

NO KING OF ENGLAND has ever been regarded by his contemporaries as an absolute monarch. The very concept is unknown in English law. When the phrase 'absolute king' was used, as it was (for instance) about King Henry VIII, it meant only that the king of England had no overlord, or in other words that England was an independent kingdom. Internally he could not be an absolute king because he was always subject to the law. Indeed, at the time of Magna Carta the powers which we now know as the royal prerogatives were more often known as the king's liberties. They were liberties of the same kind as the liberties of the Church, the barons, and all free men. Like those other liberties they came from the law.

This theory of the predominance of law can be traced back to the very foundations of England, for the Germanic tribes which settled in the southern half of Britain and created Angleland or England were not subjects of imperial Rome and knew nothing of Roman law. They brought with them their customary laws; and the essence of customary law is the general acceptance of mutual rights and obligations. The rights and obligations of an old English king were the converse of the obligations and rights of other Englishmen. The Norman Conquest in 1066 did not alter this general proposition. Indeed, it was reinforced by the ideas of the Normans. William of Normandy claimed to be the successor of Edward the Confessor and undertook to maintain his laws, which were the customary laws of England. In Normandy, especially under Duke William, feudal ideas had developed more strongly than in England. The essence of feudal law was the mutual relations of lord and man. It was the duty of the lord to maintain and protect the rights of his men.

The accusation against King John was that he had stretched his liberties so far that they infringed the liberties of the Church, the barons, the cities and boroughs, and free men generally. Magna Carta was, fundamentally, an assertion of the principle of the predominance of law. The word *libertas* or liberty often means a privilege, such as a right to exercise jurisdiction in a county, conferred by grant or prescription. The

13

Norman French word was not *liberté* but *franchise*, and in the modern law a liberty is usually called a franchise. The liberties in Magna Carta are not franchises of this kind. Cap. 1 ends with the sentence: 'We have also granted to all the free men of our kingdom, for ourselves and our heirs for ever, all the liberties written below, to be had and held by them and their heirs from us and our heirs for ever.' The liberties which follow are, however, propositions of law relating to matters in respect of which King John was thought to have exceeded his legal powers.

The liberties of England are thus principles of English law. The word is used in the same sense in such phrases as 'the liberties of the subject', 'the laws and liberties of England', and 'fundamental liberties'. These are some of the laws which bind the king, his ministers, officers and judges. The king, too, had liberties or prerogatives which imposed duties on his subjects; but, like the liberties of his subjects, they were conferred, circumscribed and protected by the law. As Bracton said about the middle of the thirteenth century, 'the king should not be under man, but under God and the Law'.

The liberties of England specified in Magna Carta must seem, to the modern reader, to be a very odd collection, and for the most part they are obsolete. If Magna Carta were redrafted in the form of an Act of Parliament it would contain four Parts. Part I would be a single clause from Cap. 1, protecting the rights and liberties of the English Church. It was and is—for it is still in force—so general in its terms that it has never been very important. Indeed, though its primary purpose was to forbid interference by the king in relation to ecclesiastical benefices and other ecclesiastical property, some eighteenth-century lawyers thought that it was designed to prevent interference by the Pope.

Part II would contain fourteen provisions relating to the services and incidents of the feudal tenure of land. The tenure of land was, however, profoundly affected by the statute *Quia Emptores* in 1290, and feudal tenures were abolished, from 1645, by the Statute of Tenures of 1660. Though Magna Carta had a considerable influence on the development of the law relating to land, there would be nothing in Part II which would be relevant to modern conditions.

Part III would contain fourteen provisions relating to the administration of justice. Three of these, Caps. 8, 14 and 29, are still in force. Most of the provisions were obsolete before the end of the thirteenth century because of the reforms effected by King Edward I. It is, however, on this Part that emphasis would be placed, not only because it would include the famous Cap. 29, but also because there are implications in other provisions which have proved to be of fundamental importance.

Part IV would contain the remaining nine provisions, of which five are still in force. Only a few—of which Cap. 30 allowing (foreign) merchants freely to pass the ports is the most notable—have had permanent importance.

It is, however, plain that the insistence of Lords and Commons for nearly two hundred years that Magna Carta be confirmed and observed was due not to its content but to its implications. Cap. 29 was important even in the fourteenth century because it was concerned so essentially with the liberty of the subject. The substance of the petition that the Charters be confirmed and kept was, however, that the laws of England be maintained and be observed by the king and by the great men as by others. Magna Carta was the symbol of what we should now call the Rule of Law, Government according to Law, or constitutional government. Though they were not aware of it, the men of the fourteenth and early fifteenth centuries were laying the foundations of constitutional government. The word 'constitution' was not used, in the sense of a framework of government, before the seventeenth century. It came into use at the beginning of that century because of the development of parliamentary institutions under the Tudors. The maintenance of constitutional government requires, however, the maintenance of the laws in general. What the men of the fourteenth century knew from their own experience was that the liberties of England, which mean the liberties of all free men—and by the seventeenth century all Englishmen were free men—depended on the observance of law by king, lord and commoner alike. Without law there is no liberty.

III Magna Carta and Parliament

THERE IS NOTHING ABOUT PARLIAMENT in Magna Carta because in 1215 or 1225 the institution did not exist. It is difficult to speak of it as an institution until permanent machinery was built up and records were kept in the sixteenth century. The official record of the medieval parliaments was the Statute Roll; but the statutes were drafted by the judges and approved by the King in Council, usually after the parliaments had been dissolved. There were other records, not all of which have survived, and those which have survived have enabled the historians to build up a history of Parliament as an institution.

It has sometimes been suggested that Caps. 12 and 14 of King John's Charter of 1215 provide one of the main sources. They required that no scutage* or aid, except the customary aids, be imposed 'unless by the common counsel of our kingdom'; and to obtain the common counsel of the kingdom writs should be issued severally to the archbishops, bishops, abbots, earls and greater barons, while other tenants of the Crown were to be summoned through the sheriffs and bailiffs. It need hardly be said that, in a constitution which is built up from precedent to precedent, every precedent helps. It has to be observed, however, that these provisions were not inserted in the Charters of 1216, 1217 and 1225. They were known to later generations only because one of the chroniclers, Matthew Paris, included them in his text of Magna Carta, which was in other respects the text of 1225. Nor were they observed. In the fourteenth century subsidies were usually approved in parliament, but the medieval parliaments consisted not of tenants of the Crown, but of the archbishops, bishops, abbots, earls and barons to whom were added representatives of the counties and the boroughs. This evolution, too, was from precedent to precedent. The representatives of the counties first appeared in 1227; representatives of the boroughs may have appeared in 1237, and some certainly appeared in Simon de Montfort's parliament of 1265. In and after the reign of Edward I representatives of the commons were usually present.

* Money paid by a feudal holder of land to his lord in lieu of personal service

16

This peaceful scene is the River Thames flowing past the meadow of Runnymede. It was here that King John sealed the document usually known as Magna Carta in 1215, the year before his death

Below left The Great Seal of King John. *Below right* The head of King John's effigy in Worcester Cathedral, where he requested in his will that his body should lie

Obverse

Reverse

Simon de Montfort's seal, a reproduction from the original in the Bibliothèque Nationale in Paris. There are other seals in the British Museum in London, but apart from a window in Chartres Cathedral (*see outside back cover*) these are the only existing contemporary portrayals of Simon

The first surviving writ of summons to a parliament. This writ, dated December 1274, was addressed to the Sheriff of Buckinghamshire and Bedfordshire and summoned representatives of boroughs and cities to attend the parliament of Easter 1275. The names of some of the representatives are written on the reverse side of the writ, while others are to be found on the return which is attached to it

This, the earliest picture of the House of Commons, during the last
Parliament of King James I in 1624, shows clearly the ancestry of the
present House. The Speaker is in his chair, the clerks are at the table.
The seating, as now, was insufficient for all the Members. The figure
kneeling at the bar in the foreground is being reprimanded for having
infringed one of the privileges of the House and is in the custody of the
Serjeant-at-Arms who carries the Mace

Milites Provinciarum & Burgenſes (quos vocant) utrinq̃, qui Cameram Parlamenti inferiorem conſtituunt, Prolocutorem conducentes.

Though the buildings housing Parliament may have changed with the years, Parliament itself preserves a striking continuity, not only of purpose but also of ceremony and even outward appearance. In the left-hand picture Queen Elizabeth I confirms, in 1584, the election of a new Speaker. The Commons are seen at the bar in the foreground, while the Lords, spiritual and temporal, occupy the benches in the body of the House. The Woolsack, traditional seat of the Lord Chancellor, is vacant because, in the presence of the Queen, the Chancellor relinquishes his position of authority. In the right-hand picture, taken nearly four hundred years later, in 1964, the similarity is easily seen, and although the camera angle excludes them, the Commons Members are in fact gathered at the bar of the House behind the phalanx of Lords, who face Queen Elizabeth II as she opens a new session of Parliament

v

The Courts of Justice in Westminster Hall. Before 1215 the judges followed the Sovereign round the land so that justice could be done wherever he was. Magna Carta provided that private suits (common pleas) should be held in some certain place. This resulted in the Court of Common Pleas' being established in Westminster Hall. It was followed by the Court of King's Bench (*seen on the left*) and the Court of Chancery (*on the right*). In an adjacent room was the Court of Exchequer, which originally dealt with revenue cases but extended its jurisdiction to cover the common law. The public was admitted at all times, and there was always a great throng of people—booksellers, lawyers, clients and others. Justice at common law and in equity was thus administered openly and publicly

Opposite upper This document in Charles I's handwriting sets out the King's instructions for the impeachment of five leaders of the Opposition in the House of Commons (Hampden, Pym, Holles, Hazlerigg and Strode), charging them with activities 'subverting . . . the government of England'. Shortly afterwards the King attempted to take them by force (*opposite lower*). The entrance of the King into the House of Commons was an affront to precedent, and that it was with armed men made matters still worse. This was one of the acts that led to civil war and so to the King's execution in 1649. Thus the spirit of the original Charters of John and Henry in the thirteenth century was still, four hundred years later, being preserved—and the liberties of the people (represented by the House of Commons) guarded against undue pressure

1 You ar to accuse those ~~[deleted]~~ joyntlie & seuerallie

2 you ar to reserue the power of making additionalls

3 When the Comitie for examination is a naming (wch you
must presse to be close & under tey of secresie) if eather
Essex, Warwick, Holland, Say, ~~[deleted]~~ Wharton, or
Brooke be named, you must desyre that they may be spared
because you ar to examine them as witnesses for me

After the execution of Charles I the House of Commons claimed the power of the whole Parliament, set up a Council of State and established a Commonwealth. In 1650 Cromwell became Lord General and in 1653, during a debate in the House, he called in his troops and forcibly dissolved the House. This Dutch satirical drawing shows the troops dismissing the Members and lifting the Speaker out of his chair. Though there were 'Parliaments' during the Commonwealth and the Protectorate, soon after Cromwell's death the Army recalled the Long Parliament. When the Members who had been excluded in 1648 by Pride's Purge rejoined the House it voted for free elections. The Parliament so elected voted for the return of Charles II, as shown in the lower picture

The presence of the commons in parliament was important in the evolution of Magna Carta because it provided opportunities for drawing attention to the liberties of England. The draftsmen of King John's charter realized that the principal difficulty was to induce the king to observe it. They therefore provided for the election of twenty-five barons who would have power to enforce the provisions of the Charter. This provision was not repeated in the later Charters. The observance of Magna Carta was sought to be ensured by requiring the sheriffs to read it in the county courts four times a year and by requiring the bishops to pronounce anathemas, twice a year, against those who failed to observe its provisions. Publicity of this kind was essential before the development of printing put copies of Magna Carta into every private library; but the fact that the men of the county knew its provisions did not necessarily result in obedience to the law; and even the anathemas pronounced by the bishops did not necessarily ensure that its provisions were observed by the king and his ministers. In the reigns of Edward III and Richard II (1327–99) Magna Carta was confirmed by twenty-four statutes. On other occasions the Commons petitioned that the Charters be confirmed, and the petition received the royal assent, but no statute was made.

There were, too, important developments of Magna Carta in *Confirmatio Cartarum* (1297), *Articuli super Cartas* (1300), and in seven of the statutes of Edward III (1327–1377). Among them was the famous 'due process' clause which provided the precedent for the 5th and 14th Amendments to the Constitution of the United States:

> No man of what estate or condition that he be, shall be put out of land or tenement, nor taken nor imprisoned, nor disinherited, nor put to death, without being brought in answer by due process of law (28 Edward III, Cap. 3, 1354).

This was one of the 'seven statutes', of which the first was Magna Carta, quoted in the most famous debate on the liberties of England. Sir Thomas Darnel and four other knights refused to pay the forced loans to which they had been assessed in accordance with the commands of King Charles I. They were imprisoned and took out writs of *habeas corpus* in order that they might be released on bail. Because the court refused to bail them, there were a great debate in the House of Commons and conferences with the House of Lords. The debates led to the drafting of the Petition of Right, 1628, by Sir Edward Coke. The king gave it a reluctant assent.

The ultimate remedy against a recalcitrant king was rebellion. Under feudal law it was actually lawful, and the events which led to King John's Charter of 1215 began with a formal 'defiance', or repudiation of allegiance, by some of the barons. Edward II (1327) and Richard II (1399) were deposed in parliament, Charles I was executed after a civil war (1649) and James II was declared by Act of Parliament to have abdicated (1688). The Queen now holds her title by Act of Parliament, the Act of Settlement (1701) as amended by His Majesty's Declaration of Abdication Act, 1936.

In a constitutional sense the Civil War of 1642–60 was salutary. It caused far less desolation than a modern civil war would do, but inevitably it disrupted the lives of those ordinary people who managed to survive it, and many did not. Though there were periods of relative peace, it lasted eighteen years; and in the perspective of history it seems to be a series of *coups*. The tyranny of the 'saints' was worse than the tyranny of the Stuarts because it affected ordinary people more closely. Government by the army was so unpopular that even in the twentieth century the army has to be legalized by resolution of both Houses of Parliament every year. Above all, it was realized that obedience to the law required obedience to all the laws. Though it is true that a revolution or *coup d'état* changed only the constitutional law and the general law was left unaltered, its compulsive force was necessarily weakened. Those who obtained power by unlawful means had the armed forces behind them, but they destroyed the sense of security upon which obedience to law was founded. Our liberty does not depend only on the Metropolitan Police, the magistrates in Bow Street, the judges of the Supreme Court, the Brigade of Guards, the Home Secretary, or even the Queen, though they all help; it depends also on 'the man on the Clapham omnibus'—which goes down the Strand to Whitehall and Westminster—the ordinary reasonable man.

This produces the doctrine which has been called the doctrine of constitutional continuity, the doctrine that, though constitutional changes may be necessary, as indeed the recent history of the Commonwealth shows, they ought to be effected by constitutional means. Even in 1660, when the legislation of the Long Parliament prevented the summoning of a lawful Parliament by Charles II, an effort was made to stick as close to the law as the law allowed; and the Revolution of 1688 was made to look lawful even though it clearly was not. A few unlawful acts were rendered necessary by the mental illnesses of George III, but otherwise constitutional continuity has been maintained in England, and in all territories over which Parliament has had jurisdiction, since the Bill of Rights of 1689.

Much of the legislation of the fourteenth and fifteenth centuries was concerned with taxation. Though two of the ancient forms of taxation, scutages and aids, were dealt with in King John's Charter of 1215, there was nothing about it in the Magna Carta of 1225. On the other hand, the freedom of property rights protected by Cap. 29 was of little value if the king could impose heavy taxation at his discretion. Though it was and still is the law that a tax on property is not a diminution of property rights, this is a very legalistic interpretation, because in fact taxation must be met out of property. For the same reason Cap. 14 of Magna Carta, which is still in force, forbids excessive fines.

The medieval Commons were concerned especially with customs duties. They were called customs because certain duties on wool, wool-fels and leather were leviable by ancient custom having the force of law. When the kings' wars caused them to be more than usually short of money, they frequently resorted to the device of increasing the duties. On occasions the assent of a parliament was given, sometimes *ex post facto*. A first attempt at prohibition was made in the 'statute' of 1297 known as *Confirmatio Cartarum* which arose out of a petition, not in parliament but in an assembly of landowners summoned by King Edward I in order to raise money.

Confirmatio Cartarum required that no aid or duty be raised without the 'common assent of the whole kingdom', and later lawyers read this as a reference to parliament. This was not intended, and Edward I continued to negotiate separately with the Church, the landowners, the boroughs and the merchants. It was in the next century that the principle was established that taxation must be voted by the Commons of England in parliament assembled. Even this development did not settle the question of the

19

customs, for it was thought by some of the royal lawyers that the levying of duties was incidental to the prerogative power to control relations with foreign countries. The court so decided in 1606 in the case of John Bate, a Levantine merchant, who refused to pay an additional customs duty levied by order of King James I. The result of the decision was that the rates of duty were again increased. In 1628 the Commons had to deal with forced loans as well as customs duties, and the Petition of Right, 1628, provided that 'no man hereafter be compelled to make or yield any gift, loan benevolence, tax, or such like charge, without common consent by Act of Parliament'.

This provision did not stop King Charles I from raising the peculiar tax known as ship-money (though it was claimed not to be a tax). John Hampden refused to pay the 20s. to which he was assessed, but the court upheld the validity of ship-money by a narrow majority. That decision was reversed by Act of the Long Parliament in 1641 as 'contrary to and against the laws and statutes of this realm, the right of property, the liberty of the subject, former resolutions in Parliament, and the Petition of Right . . .'.

What is called 'The Eleven Years Tyranny' from 1629 to 1640, when King Charles I tried to govern without a parliament, showed that a king of England could not 'live on his own', even by pressing his prerogative powers beyond what most lawyers thought to be legal. This was even more obvious to Charles II, because the revenues from military tenures disappeared in 1645; and, though the Ordinance was regarded as invalid because it had not received the royal assent, it had to be confirmed by the Statute of Tenures of 1660. Reliance had, therefore, to be placed on taxation voted in Parliament; and this became quite clear after 1688.

Parliamentary control of taxation did not prevent heavy taxation, but it did prevent arbitrary taxation. Also, parliamentary control of legislation had developed side by side with parliamentary control of taxation. After 1688, no legislation could be passed, taxation raised, or armed forces maintained, without the authority of Parliament. The great debates in the Parliaments of James I and Charles I had created the tradition that Parliament, and especially the House of Commons, was the guardian of English and, after the union with Scotland, of British liberty.

20

The various groups of politicians who called themselves Whigs considered themselves to be the advocates and supporters of liberty. Though we now know, through the researches of Mr. Peter Laslett, that John Locke's two *Treatises of Civil Government* were not written as a defence of the Revolution Settlement of 1688, the book was an exposition of the political philosophy acceptable to the Whigs, the 'principles of 1688'.

Locke's liberty was liberty according to law. 'Freedom', he said, 'is not what Sir Robert Filmer tells us, "a liberty for every one to do what he lists, to live as he pleases, and not to be tied by any laws"; but freedom of men under government is to have a standing rule to live by, common to every one of that society, and made by the legislative power erected in it.' This brings us back, however, to Magna Carta, for the liberties of England are liberties under the law. The essential principle of Magna Carta, as has already been emphasized, was that the laws should be maintained. We shall see presently how the laws so developed after 1225 that 'the laws and liberties of England' became a standard formula, showing the essential alliance of law and liberty. After 1688, however, the protection of the liberties of England rested with Parliament and especially with the House of Commons, for the legislative power—legislative power exercised in accordance with the law and custom of Parliament but unlimited by any written constitution—was vested in the King in Parliament. However perfect the devices for the protection of liberty developed by the common law, they were ineffective if the King in Parliament enacted laws which infringed the liberties of England.

It is easy to find examples of encroachment. The most obvious are the notorious 'Six Acts' of 1819. The French wars having ended with a victory at Waterloo, a period of rapid adaptation to peace-time conditions set in. In this period of economic and social disturbance the population was particularly susceptible to Radical agitation for reforms in Church and State. Though there had been no cause to fear a British Revolution of the type of the French Revolution of 1789, the considerable population which industrialization had brought to the towns to live in conditions of squalor and economic insecurity seemed to many of the wealthier classes to be a considerable danger to the stability of society. The system of representation which had been reasonably satisfactory under

21

Queen Anne had become anomalous under the Prince Regent, though it was not changed until 1832. In general, England (and, still more, Scotland) was under-governed. Also, it was virtually un-policed, for the arrangements for keeping the peace in the villages and commercial towns were entirely inadequate in the great towns, and above all in London. For information about potential civil disturbances the Home Office relied upon the secret reports of informers, many of whom took care that their reports did not lack colour. If rioting did break out the only recourse was to call out armed forces.

The general disturbance after Waterloo, the exaggerated reports of informers, the recollections of the Terror in Paris, and the general fear of 'the mob', were already creating perturbation when 'Orator' Hunt addressed a meeting of 60,000 people on St Peter's Field, Manchester. The crowd was unarmed, but the magistrates thought that it was the beginning of an insurrection and called in the cavalry, whose operations caused the loss of some lives and many injuries.

The Six Acts were the response of the Government and Parliament to a situation which in modern Manchester would have been dealt with by a police inspector and a posse of constables without special powers of any kind. The absurdity of what was satirically called 'Peterloo' became apparent as it receded into history. When Sir Robert Peel became Home Secretary (for the second time) in 1828 he chose the remedy, which was not so obvious then as it is now, of a professional force of unarmed police with the ordinary powers of a constable at common law. The experiment, tried in the metropolis, proved to be a success and was extended to the whole United Kingdom. Special powers are certainly needed where there is an organized effort to bring the law into contempt, and special powers are needed in conditions of 'total war' (as in Britain in 1914–18 and 1939–45). The exact balance between police powers and public liberties has to vary from time to time; in the traffic conditions of modern London, for instance, a public demonstration by an organized group of political partisans has to be regulated and, frequently, forbidden because it is, and indeed is usually intended to be, a public nuisance. The common law has had to be reinforced by legislation to meet changing conditions.

Apart from the law, however, the citizen has the protection of the two Houses of Parliament. The fundamental principles of Magna Carta, as elaborated by legislation and the common law, have become part of the common stock of ideas; they are principles accepted by social convention. They are frequently articulated by lawyers; for others they are more often inarticulate major premises. The Latin of Cap. 29 has been translated into the language of the back streets. Members of Parliament and peers of the realm share these common notions or prejudices and give effect to them by motions and speeches. The House of Commons is at its best when it deals with what appears to be an injustice. Criticism seldom comes from one side of the House only, but the fact that in both Houses of Parliament there is an organized Opposition is of profound importance. There are other ways of protecting the fundamental liberties, as the United States of America constantly demonstrates; but the combination of responsible government and political opposition is particularly effective.

In the British system nearly all legislation emanates from the Ministries of the Crown and has the approval of the Cabinet. The instructions upon which drafting is based are drawn up by civil servants, but the drafting is done by professional lawyers of long experience. These lawyers share the prejudices of their colleagues at the Bar and on the Bench. The civil servants are more concerned with the policy behind the proposed legislation; but one of their principal duties is to foresee and guard against avoidable criticism of their Minister in the Houses of Parliament. Criticism in matters of policy is usually to be expected, for it is the task of the Opposition to point out and emphasize what they regard as defects in the draft legislation. On matters of civil liberty, however, the Opposition's case has much sympathy among the Government's own supporters. Ministers do not like provisions which they have difficulty in defending; still less do they like provisions which they cannot adequately defend and have to withdraw or amend because of the 'sense of the House' even though they would get a majority if they put them to the vote. The combination of a draftsman with all the prejudices of an English lawyer and a civil servant anxious to protect his Minister from parliamentary 'trouble' is usually effective in preventing draft legislation from proposing encroachments upon fundamental liberties. If it happens not to be effective, however, the obnoxious provisions have to run the gauntlet in two Houses, in both of which Her Majesty's Opposition are delighted to find fault with the proposals of Her Majesty's Government. In the House of Lords, too, there are many cross-bench peers, not actively associated with any political party, who think it their duty to emphasize non-political defects in proposals for legislation. At least a dozen of them are judges, who carefully maintain their impartiality in matters of politics, but whose criticisms have the more force for that reason.

The protection of the fundamental liberties is not, however, solely a question of preventing encroachment by legislation. The government of 53 million people in a highly industrialized society requires a complex apparatus of government, in which injustice may be committed at any administrative level where Government and people meet. Her Majesty's Government is technically responsible only for actions and decisions taken under powers conferred on the Queen or her Ministers: but thousands of people are exercising those powers every day and it would be surprising if there were not occasional lapses from the high standards which parliamentary control enjoins. Even where the Government is technically not responsible, however, it can take action, if necessary with the approval of both Houses of Parliament. Much of the government of Great Britain is in the hands of elected local authorities. Outside London the police are under the control of watch committees formed by representatives of local authorities and justices of the peace. Neither the Home Secretary's control of the Metropolitan Police nor the watch committee's control of its police force extends to the giving of orders about the enforcement of the law, for the constable is an officer of the law with independent powers controlled by the courts of law. Nevertheless, if there is a serious mis-carriage of justice—serious in relation to the individual affected, whether or not it is of political importance—Government and Parliament are concerned.

There is a standard technique for such cases. The first step is to inform a Member of Parliament. He communicates with the appropriate Minister. In many cases that Minister will at once institute an inquiry. If he thinks that a formal tribunal ought to be established and he cannot confer the necessary powers to take evidence on oath, he puts down a motion in both

Houses for a tribunal of inquiry. If, however, the action of the Minister seems to the Member to be inadequate, he puts down a question for oral answer in the House. If the Member thinks that the Minister's answer is unsatisfactory, he may indicate that he proposes to raise the matter on the adjournment—a procedure which results in a debate of half an hour at the end of public business in the House of Commons. In a really serious case, however, the Member will, at the end of the question hour, ask leave to move the adjournment for the consideration of 'a definite matter of urgent public importance'. If Mr Speaker considers that it falls within that category and forty members rise to support the request, it is granted. Since Her Majesty's Opposition is present in force, the support is usually more than adequate. The motion is then debated the same evening. There is a flurry in Whitehall in order to brief the Minister. If he cannot make a good case he has to admit it and to establish the tribunal which, if he had been better advised, he would have established already.

The complaint which starts this parliamentary activity need not have arisen out of an illegal action. If it was illegal there is a remedy at law, and Parliament would not interfere if legal proceedings had already begun. The action may, however, have been legal but unconscionable; and in that case there is no remedy save in Parliament. The effect of parliamentary activity is, however, to broaden the liberties protected by law. An action by a Minister, a civil servant or a police constable may be lawful. In the eyes of the House of Commons or a tribunal of inquiry it may nevertheless be wrong. If it is, and a Minister is responsible—and he is responsible for the actions of civil servants in his Ministry—he will offer his resignation and, if he really has been at fault, by negligence or otherwise, his resignation will be accepted and, probably, his political career for ever terminated. Since no Minister is responsible for the actions of a police constable, the latter will be reprimanded by a senior officer and may find it desirable to resign.

The key to the parliamentary situation is Her Majesty's Opposition. It deliberately organizes criticism of Government legislation. It gives support to any Member, of whatever party, who thinks that he has discovered a case of unconscionable behaviour. This is part of the job confided to it by some two hundred years of history. Like other British institutions it was built up from precedent to precedent, and therefore it had no precise beginning. It is usual, however, to regard Charles James Fox as the first Leader of the Opposition and to give the date 1783, when young William Pitt became Prime Minister at the age of 24. The Opposition is so much an institution of the British Constitution that since 1937 the Leader of the Opposition has received an official salary, charged on the Consolidated Fund by permanent legislation so that an annual vote may not be required, as it is for Ministerial salaries. In 1965 the Queen in Parliament, by a coincidence, has celebrated the 700th anniversary of Simon de Montfort's parliament by raising the salary of the Leader of the Opposition in the House of Commons, conferring a salary on the Leader of the Opposition in the House of Lords, and providing salaries for the Chief Opposition Whips in both Houses.

IV Magna Carta and the Common Law

CAP. 11 OF MAGNA CARTA (Cap. 17 of King John's Charter) provided that 'common pleas shall not follow our Court, but shall be held in some certain place'. Cap. 17 of Magna Carta (Cap. 24 of King John's Charter) provided that 'no sheriff, constable, coroners, or others of our bailiffs, shall hold pleas of our crown'.

Common pleas are pleas between citizens and cover the greater part of private law. Pleas of the crown are usually criminal proceedings taken in the name of the Queen and therefore cover the greater part of the criminal law. The two branches of the law, taken together, were what medieval lawyers meant by the common law. Though the medieval phrasing hides the fact, the two provisions are the first formal step in the development of the independence of the judiciary.

It need hardly be said that the draftsmen of Magna Carta had no such intention. Royal judges were royal servants, appointed and dismissed by the king at his pleasure. The king himself could sit in his own court and give judgment, and King John frequently did so. The king could also give orders to his judges about cases coming before them when he was not present. It had not occurred to King John's barons that any other arrangement was possible. Cap. 11 was designed for the convenience of suitors in cases in which the king had no special interest. If the judges went round the country with the king, the suitors could get justice only by going where the king happened to be, assuming that they could find out where he was. It was therefore desired that some judges should hear common pleas in some certain place. The provision was observed, a number of judges were separated from the judges following the king and they formed the Common Bench. With occasional variations in the fourteenth century, the 'certain place' was Westminster Hall (where the body of Sir Winston Churchill lay in state before his funeral on 30 January 1965).

The judges who followed the king were called the King's Bench; when the king was an infant or was in the neighbourhood of Westminster (as he usually was) the King's Bench sat in Westminster Hall; and in due course they ceased to follow the king and sat permanently in West-

27

minster Hall. Civil proceedings before the king's judges began with a royal writ issued from the royal chancery. It was therefore convenient for the chancery, which developed a jurisdiction in law and equity and became the Court of Chancery, to be located in Westminster Hall. Finally, the barons of the Exchequer, who originally dealt only with cases arising out of the royal revenues, developed a jurisdiction at common law and in equity by using the fiction that the suitor was the king's debtor and was unable to pay his debt because the defendant would not pay up. Since the barons were royal judges like their brothers on the benches, the Court of Exchequer sat, not in Westminster Hall, but in a room accessible from it.

It is also relevant that both the King's Bench and the Common Bench developed the practice of relying on a jury to decide questions of fact. There is nothing about trial by jury in Magna Carta, but later lawyers read it into Cap. 29. *Per legale judicium parium suorum* is, literally, by the lawful judgment of their peers (or equals). The members of a jury are the peers of the defendant. Therefore, it was thought, Cap. 29 required trial by jury in all cases at common law. Though the historians convince us that trial by jury was not in Magna Carta, our learned predecessors said that it was, and what our learned predecessors said is the law of England.

Trial by jury requires that an advocate explain to the jury, orally, the nature of his client's case. He then produces his witnesses and examines them orally, in order that the jury may hear. The advocate for the other side has then to cross-examine the witnesses in order to put a different complexion on the case. After all the witnesses for the plaintiff or the prosecution have been called, the advocate for the defendant explains his client's case to the jury and examines his witnesses, who may be cross-examined. Finally the judge or judges, who act as umpires between the advocates, listen to legal argument and then explain the law to the jury, sum up the evidence to them, and leave them to consider their verdict.

This was 'due process' at the common law, as required by the statute of 1354 already quoted, and as administered in Westminster Hall. But Westminster Hall was a place of public resort. The court was separated from the public by a bar. The advocate was called a serjeant-at-law, and serjeant means servant: the serjeant served the law as well as his client. Serjeants have been succeeded by Queen's Counsel, whose duty it is to serve both the Queen and the law, a double duty which raises no conflict because it is the Queen's duty to see that the law is observed and justice is done. Like their predecessors the serjeants they are 'called within the bar'. The serjeants had assistants or apprentices who stood at the bar and were called 'utter' (or outer) 'barristers'. They were, and still are, 'called to the Bar'. To learn the law it was necessary to stand at the bar and listen to the exposition of the law by the judges and the serjeants. Since these discussions were ephemeral, barristers frequently took notes and wrote them up in 'year books' which could be sold to barristers and even to serjeants and judges. The result is that England has a remarkable series of 'law reports' which extend from the latter part of the thirteenth century to the present day.

The judges, serjeants and barristers lived in inns and hostels between the City of Westminster and the City of London. They dined together, argued together (some of Sir Edward Coke's Reports relate to post-prandial discussions in Serjeants' Inn), and developed a professional *esprit de corps*. Serjeants' Inn disappeared with the serjeants, and the judges now remain in their Inns, of which there are four, the Inner and Middle Temples in the former home of the Knights Templar, and Lincoln's Inn and Gray's Inn, off High Holborn. Precedence is determined, not by office but by elevation to the Bench, so that a Queen's Counsel, or even a barrister, may be senior to a Lord of Appeal. The Inns have complete discretion to call a student to the Bar and, subject to appeal to the High Court, to disbar a barrister. Professional etiquette is very strict, and is designed not only to maintain the prestige and dignity of the member of the profession—emoluments are never discussed by the Benches of the Inns—but also to maintain the prestige and dignity of the law.

Justice was administered in Westminster Hall openly by a procedure which required that every document be read and every word be spoken in public. The observations of the judges, and the charges which they delivered to the juries, might be taken down in writing and quoted against their professional reputation. In the middle ages they could still receive the king's commands, but it was usually necessary to explain them in public. It was inevitable that the judges should develop a remarkable independence with the support of their colleagues within and at the bar.

29

As late as the seventeenth century Sir Edward Coke, as Chief Justice, informed the king that he might sit in the King's Bench, but he added that he must give judgment through the mouths of his judges. In *Darnel's Case* in 1627 the judges adjourned the application for bail because they wished to consult the king in accordance with precedent, but they were severely criticized, and actually appeared to defend themselves, in Parliament. The validity of the writs of ship-money was certified by the judges before the writs were issued, but *John Hampden's Case* was decided in open court and the judges were divided; the decision of the majority was ultimately reversed in Parliament. Sir Edward Coke was dismissed by James I in 1616, and there were later dismissals of judges. But the fate of 'tough old Coke, the toughest man England ever knew' was remembered. The Act of Settlement, 1701, provided that judges should hold their commissions, not at the king's pleasure, but during good behaviour, though they might be removed after addresses by both Houses of Parliament. No judge has in fact been removed since 1701, and the judges administer justice 'freely and fairly, without favour and without fear'.

This was not the intention, but it was the result of Cap. 11 of Magna Carta. Justice was, however, administered not merely in Westminster Hall, but also locally. Cap. 17 was concerned primarily with this local administration in county and London courts. The justices in eyre, who were succeeded by the justices of assize, went round on circuit (eyre = *iter* = journey) to supervise the local administration of justice. In the course of their journeys they heard both common pleas and pleas of the Crown, as the justices of assize do to this day. Before the author as he writes is an intimation from the Vice-Chancellor of the University of Cambridge, advising the Heads of Colleges, the University Officers and others that on 26 February 1965, at 10 a.m. he will leave the Senate House to 'wait upon the Judges [of Assize] on their arrival in Cambridge'. One of the Judges of Assize will be the High Sheriff of Cambridgeshire, and he will actually hear pleas of the Crown contrary to Cap. 17 of Magna Carta (which has been repealed), but he will observe the principle by taking no part in the proceedings. Local justice was formerly supervised by the King in Council, but that jurisdiction was for all practical purposes removed by the Long Parliament in 1641. Inferior courts are in theory supervised by the Judges of Assize but in practice by the Supreme Court of Judicature in the Strand, London, which has succeeded to the powers of the Court of King's Bench exercised in Westminster Hall. Local justice is thus as independent of Crown and Government as the justice administered in the Strand.

Until 1641, however, the justice administered or controlled in Westminster Hall was in competition with justice administered in other jurisdictions whose traditions had been set not by Westminster Hall but by the Roman law. The ecclesiastical courts had a wide jurisdiction over laymen as well as over clerks in holy orders. The concept of liberty of conscience is not to be found in Magna Carta and was accepted with great reluctance after 1688. The writ *de haeretico comburendo*, under which persons condemned as heretics by the ecclesiastical courts could be burned at the stake, was abolished in 1677. In effect, however, those courts had lost their jurisdiction over laymen in 1641.

The Court of Admiralty had jurisdiction on the high seas and administered justice according to the Roman law, its practitioners being 'civilians' from Oxford and Cambridge. Unlike the ecclesiastical courts, however, it could be kept within its jurisdiction by writs issued from the King's Bench. Since the civilians also practised in, and were, after Queen Elizabeth I, judges of, ecclesiastical courts, they maintained a modest existence in Doctors Commons until 1859, though by that time most of them were also barristers.

Much more important was the Council and some of its Tudor offshoots, particularly the notorious Court of Star Chamber. The Council exercised the jurisdiction remaining in the king after the other royal courts had achieved a measure of independence, and it included the king's jurisdiction to regulate those courts. Both civilians and common lawyers took part in its work, but so did the king himself, bishops and laymen, usually peers. It used, not the procedure of the common law, but the 'inquisitorial' procedure, founded on the Roman law, which is still used in many countries. In the right hands it is an excellent procedure and has some advantages over common law procedure, though it also has disadvantages. Indeed, even the Court of Star Chamber, which was in origin the Council sitting in the Star Chamber in the absence of the king, exercised useful functions for most of the sixteenth century. It could, and did, deal with offenders who were too powerful to be dealt with by a jury, and it developed most of the offences, including perjury, which led to injustice in trials at common law. Its notoriety, and the notoriety of Council juris-diction generally, arose from the conduct of trials for treason and con-spiracy in the Council. No lawyer can read the trial of Sir Walter Raleigh without distaste. Also, the Council, unlike the courts of common law, used torture to obtain confessions from alleged conspirators. We must remember the numerous conspiracies against Good Queen Bess, and the Gunpowder Plot which led to the trial of Guy Fawkes and others and to the annual firework displays (with the burning of the 'guy') on 5 November. We must also remember the difficulty of proving conspiracy in an un-policed and ill-organized society. Nevertheless, the Long Parlia-ment did a service when, in 1641, it abolished the Court of Star Chamber and virtually abolished the jurisdiction of the Council except for that part of it which is now exercised by the Judicial Committee of the Privy Council. The last man to be put to judicial torture in England was John Archer, the drummer who led the crowd which attacked Archbishop Laud's palace in 1640.

These events led to the hegemony of Westminster Hall. Neither the Court of Exchequer nor the Court of Chancery followed common law procedure, but the barons of the Exchequer were closely associated with the common law judges for centuries, and after 1673 the Chancellors were common lawyers. Under Lord Nottingham (1673–82) and his successors the rules of equity were formalized. For all practical purposes, therefore, the 'due process of law' which was the fourteenth-century interpretation of Cap. 29 of Magna Carta was in the seventeenth century and afterwards process at common law or in equity. The chapter applied to all men because all men were free; it was held in *Sommersett's Case* (1772) that slavery was inconsistent with the law of England and that any slave brought into this country could be set free by *habeas corpus*.

Accordingly, no man could be put to death except after trial by jury; no man could be kept in prison unless he was lawfully arrested under common law or statute or was imprisoned by order of a court of law or equity; no man's property could be taken away except by lawful

The Declaration of Rights of February 1689 ranks with Magna Carta as one of the two supreme constitutional documents of English history. Drawn up by the Commons and amended by the Lords, it caused a heated discussion during which it may well be that a bottle of ink was upset on the document. It asserted the historic rights of the people, including freedom of speech in parliamentary debates. It was accepted by the Prince and Princess of Orange as the terms under which they could ascend the throne. As a result they were proclaimed the same day as King and Queen jointly. Later in the year the main terms of the Declaration were incorporated in the Bill of Rights

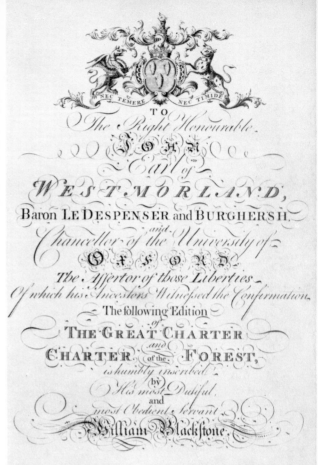

Above A great extension of British liberties was the judgment in 1756 of Lord Chief Justice Mansfield in the case of a slave, James Sommersett. As a result of this decision many thousands of slaves, brought in by their owners from the American and West Indian colonies, were freed

Above right The dedication page of Sir William Blackstone's monumental work, published in 1759, in which he set out the distinctions, hitherto never made clear, between the Great Charters of 1215, 1216, 1217 and 1225

Further proof of the spread of the will of the people and widening sphere of Parliament—Keir Hardie (*far left*) first Labour Member of the House of Commons, (*left*) Nancy, Lady Astor, the first lady Member of Parliament, with the second, Mrs. Wintringham, on her right

Winston Churchill, most famous British parliamentarian of all, surveys the damage done to the House of Commons by enemy action during the second world war

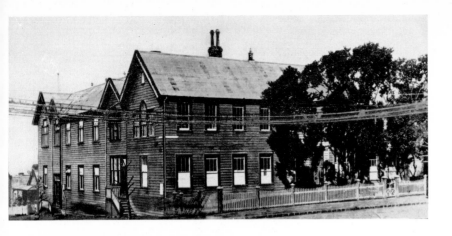

The influence of Magna Carta has spread far and wide outside Britain. It forms part of the thinking behind national constitutions of many lands, both Commonwealth and other, drawn up at different points in history: in Canada, where a convention (*opposite top*) met on Prince Edward Island in 1864 to consider the union of what were then known as the North American Colonies; in Australia, where the Australian Commonwealth was inaugurated in 1901 (*opposite bottom left*). *Above* New Zealand's constitution was drawn up in 1854 in a modest, wooden house, since demolished. In sharp contrast is the brilliant scene at Wellington when Queen Elizabeth II opened the New Zealand Parliament in 1954. *Opposite bottom right* Eminent lawyers from many countries of the Commonwealth and the United States of America came to Australia's Jubilee Law Convention held in Sydney in 1951 and by their presence showed the common source of their legal systems

QUEEN ELIZABETH II WITH THE COMMONWEALTH LEADERS

Seen from left to right   DR THE RT HON. ERIC WILLIAMS (PRIME MINISTER OF TRINIDAD AND TOBAGO)

MR SPYROS KYPRIANOU (MINISTER OF FOREIGN AFFAIRS, REPUBLIC OF CYPRUS)

DR H. K. BANDA (PRIME MINISTER—NOW PRESIDENT—OF MALAWI)

THE HON. (NOW SIR) ALBERT MARGAI (PRIME MINISTER OF SIERRA LEONE)

ALHAJI THE RT HON. SIR ABUBAKAR TAFAWA BALEWA (PRIME MINISTER OF
THE FEDERAL REPUBLIC OF NIGERIA)

YANG TERAMAT MULIA TUNKU ABDUL RAHMAN PUTRA AL-HAJ
(PRIME MINISTER OF MALAYSIA)

THE HON. JOMO KENYATTA (PRIME MINISTER—NOW PRESIDENT—OF KENYA)

THE RT HON. LESTER PEARSON (PRIME MINISTER OF CANADA)

DR THE HON. A. MILTON OBOTE (PRIME MINISTER OF UGANDA)

DURING THEIR LONDON CONFERENCE IN JULY 1964

MWALIMU JULIUS NYERERE (PRESIDENT OF THE UNITED REPUBLIC OF TANGANYIKA
AND ZANZIBAR—NOW TANZANIA)
HER MAJESTY QUEEN ELIZABETH II
THE HON. D. B. SANGSTER (DEPUTY PRIME MINISTER AND MINISTER OF FINANCE, JAMAICA)
THE RT HON. SIR ROBERT MENZIES (PRIME MINISTER OF THE COMMONWEALTH OF AUSTRALIA)
OSAGYEFO DR KWAME NKRUMAH (PRESIDENT OF THE REPUBLIC OF GHANA)
SHRI T. T. KRISHNAMACHARI (MINISTER OF FINANCE, INDIA)
SENATOR THE HON. SIRIMAVO BANDARANAIKE (THE THEN PRIME MINISTER OF CEYLON)
THE RT HON. SIR ALEC DOUGLAS-HOME, MP (THE THEN PRIME MINISTER OF THE UNITED KINGDOM)
THE RT HON. KEITH HOLYOAKE (PRIME MINISTER OF NEW ZEALAND)
FIELD-MARSHAL MOHAMMAD AYUB KHAN (PRESIDENT OF PAKISTAN)

Right The Magna Carta Memorial erected by the American Bar Association at Runnymede. Runnymede has also been chosen as the site of the British memorial to President Kennedy
Below A model of the proposed scheme

distraint or under authority of a court of law or equity; and so forth. The law on these and other points has been slowly developed over centuries. Magna Carta and the notes to it in Coke's *Institutes* (1642) cover 78 closely printed pages, of which Cap. 29 occupies 14 pages. But Cowell in 1607 said that 'all the law we have, is thought in some sort to depend of' (derive from) Magna Carta.

Particular reference must be made to the writ of *habeas corpus*. The seventeenth-century lawyers thought that it derived from Cap. 26 of Magna Carta (Cap. 36 of King John's Charter). The historians have shown that it did not; the writ referred to in that chapter was a means by which a person imprisoned could get bail, and this was one of the uses of *habeas corpus*. But *habeas corpus* has the much wider use of enabling a court to inquire into the lawfulness of any imprisonment and, if it is unlawful, to set the prisoner free or, if he is lawfully imprisoned, to release him on bail. Its development was, however, a consequence of Magna Carta. As Coke points out in his notes to Cap. 29, a person aggrieved by a breach of a statute is entitled at common law to an action upon the statute. *Habeas corpus* was originally a writ to get into court a person whose presence was needed for the proceedings pending before it; but different forms of the writ were invented, and one of them provided a remedy for unlawful imprisonment contrary to Cap. 29. Sir William Holdsworth's dictum that *habeas corpus* 'has come to be the most efficient protection ever invented for the liberty of the subject', is undoubtedly true wherever the Queen's writ runs. There is nothing more impressive in the whole judicial apparatus than a peremptory writ of *habeas corpus* requiring the gaoler to 'have the body' produced in court. Neglect to do so, or to make a return explaining why it is not produced, is a contempt of court.

v Magna Carta beyond the seas

CURIOUSLY ENOUGH, MAGNA CARTA seems never to have been exported to Scotland, though it was exported to Wales and Ireland. In the case of Ireland the so-called Magna Carta Hiberniae was an adaptation of King Henry's Charter of 1216. The Magna Carta of 1225 was not specifically applied to Ireland, but the various extensions of English law applied the liberties of England.

Elsewhere, the liberties of England have been exported in a variety of ways. Those Englishmen who settled beyond the seas took with them the laws and liberties of England in so far as they were applicable to the conditions of the new country. If those settlers and their descendants spread into new territories, they carried the laws and liberties with them. English common law and English statutes, so far as applicable, became the common law of the territories concerned. Thus almost the whole of the United States, all provinces of Canada except Quebec, and Australia and New Zealand received such portions of Magna Carta as were applicable to their conditions.

In many other territories English law was applied, either as a whole or in part, by Order in Council or local legislation. Even where English law has not been applied as a whole, the administration of justice has followed the English tradition in all territories which have been for any substantial period under British rule. In some cases, too, the application of English methods has been indirect. For instance, the laws of the four British colonies on the west coast of Africa were extended to the protectorates in the hinterland, so that such parts of Magna Carta as were applicable to local conditions became part of the law of The Gambia, Ghana, Nigeria and Sierra Leone. In India, Pakistan and Burma much English law was applied through the nineteenth-century codes, and English ideas were applied as 'justice, equity and good conscience' to fill gaps in the laws.

The influence of Magna Carta is, however, largely psychological. Except in the legal profession, that influence was probably not great outside the United States, Canada, Australia, New Zealand and perhaps South Africa. The exception for the legal profession is, however, a large and important one. The English pattern of Bench and Bar has not exactly been copied anywhere, for the Inns of Court are still a unique set of institutions. One must perhaps make some exception for Malta and Cyprus, which owe much to Italian, Greek and Turkish traditions, but elsewhere in the Commonwealth and in such countries outside the Commonwealth as Burma, Sudan and the Republic of South Africa, English traditions prevail. In the countries which were formerly colonies or protectorates, the judges were until recently members of the Colonial legal service, most of the barristers were members of the English Bar born in the country concerned, and most of the law schools were initially staffed by English law teachers. In countries with older legal traditions, including India, Pakistan and Ceylon as well as Canada, Australia, New Zealand, South Africa and, of course, the United States, much the same doctrine is taught as in the English law schools, and the legal literature has become international. Despite the fact that the laws of Quebec, South Africa, Rhodesia, Mauritius, the Seychelles, Malta and Ceylon are basically Roman and that in India, Pakistan, Malaysia and tropical Africa there are local laws covering many aspects of social life, the influence of English legal ideas on Bench and Bar has been profound, so that the common law world is wider than the sway of the common law itself.

Nor must it be forgotten that the doctrines which are variously called the Rule of Law, government according to law and constitutional government are in the United Kingdom maintained by parliamentary institutions as well as by judicial institutions. These parliamentary institutions, too, have been exported to all parts of the Commonwealth. They have not invariably been successful. Both in United Canada (Ontario and Quebec before 1867) and in the Australian colonies responsible government initially worked badly. It is therefore not surprising that there have been difficulties in Asia and Africa. It is much easier to draw a formal constitution putting into words the outline of the Westminster model than it is to create the environment and the complex of personal relationships which make the Westminster model work. Indeed, it is to be expected that where democratic government works well it will work with a different set of political conventions from those observed in Westminster. To speak of 'African' conventions is perhaps misleading, for it assumes that the conventions must be the same from Bathurst in The Gambia to Dar es Salaam in Tanzania. Those countries which have succeeded in maintaining the democratic system, the Rule of Law, and constitutional government have shown that different forms may be used in political institutions and political conventions. Variations from the Westminster model must be expected; what one hopes is that they will be variations which do not infringe fundamental principles.

The most important developments from Magna Carta, as interpreted through the centuries in England, have been in relation to Cap. 29. Though we should now consider that the political institutions of eighteenth-century England were subject to serious defects, the degree of civil liberty which prevailed in England after the Revolution of 1688 was thought worthy of study, particularly in France, where the old regime was in its last century. Study was not difficult, for the philosophy of the libertarian Whigs had been expressed by John Locke. It was from Locke that the doctrines of the rights of man developed; but the connection between Locke and the course of evolution which began (for all practical purposes) with King John's Charter of 1215 is plain.

The first Bill of Rights was, however, drafted not in France but in Virginia. The Virginian Declaration of Rights was approved by the House of Delegates on 12 June 1776. It was more legalistic and less polemical than the Declaration of Independence adopted on 4 July of the same year. Cap. 29 of Magna Carta appears both in article I and in article VIII. The latter reads:

> That in all capital or criminal prosecutions a man hath a right to demand the cause and nature of his accusation, to be confronted with the accusers and witnesses, to call for evidence in his favour, and to a speedy trial by an impartial jury of twelve men of his vicinage, without whose unanimous consent he cannot be found guilty; nor can he be compelled to give evidence against himself; that no man be deprived of his liberty, except by the law of the land or the judgment of his peers.

The direct quotation is in the last sentence; but the rest is a fair summary of the practice at common law as stated, for instance, in the fourth volume of Blackstone's *Commentaries*, first published in 1769.

The provision reappeared in a somewhat different form in the Fifth Amendment to the Constitution of the United States:

> No person shall be held to answer for a capital or otherwise infamous crime, unless on a presentment or indictment of a grand jury except in cases arising in the land or naval forces or in the militia, when in actual service, in time of war, or public danger, nor shall any person be subject, for the same offence to be twice put in jeopardy of life or limb nor shall be compelled, in any criminal case, to be a witness against himself, nor be deprived of life, liberty, or property without due process of law; nor shall private property be taken for public use without just compensation.

The first clause of this Amendment derives from English legislation of the fourteenth century, which became widely known because it was quoted, with Cap. 29 of Magna Carta, in the debates on *Darnel's Case*. Cap. 4 of the Statute of Provisors, 1350, after quoting Cap. 29 of Magna Carta, added, in the English translation,

> That from henceforth none shall be taken by petition or suggestion made to our Lord the King, or to his Council, unless it be by indictment or presentment of good and lawful people of the same neighbourhood where such deeds be done, in due manner, or by process made by writ original at the common law. . . .

This provision also brings in the 'due process' formula, which is plainer when it is read in the original Norman French. As has already been pointed out, however, 'due process of law' derives from the statute of 1354, which glosses Cap. 29 of Magna Carta in the following form:

> That no man of what estate or condition that he be, shall be put out of land or tenement, nor taken nor imprisoned, nor disinherited, nor put to death, without being brought in answer by due process of law.

On the other hand, the 'twice put in jeopardy' clause came, not from an enactment, but from a maxim of the common law, quoted by Blackstone, 'that no man is to be brought in jeopardy of his life, more than once, for the same offence'. Finally, the right of a person not to criminate himself was described by Lord Eldon as 'one of the most sacred principles of the law of this country'.

It is sometimes forgotten by English commentators on the Constitution of the United States that the maintenance of the fundamental liberties in that country does not depend only on the Constitution. Indeed, the Fifth Amendment does not apply to the State governments, though much the same effect was established by the Fourteenth Amendment, adopted in 1868. To the Bill of Rights in the Constitution of the United States must be added the Bills of Rights in the State constitutions. Moreover, much of the efficacy of these Bills of Rights depends upon the fact that they are in tune with the common law as adopted in the several States. Most of the provisions in the Bills of Rights derive from that common law and therefore never were mere paper propositions. They are peaks of high mountains, not clouds in the air. On the other hand, their importance as constitutional provisions cannot be denied, for constitutional enactment enables the courts of the United States (or the courts of the States in relation to State constitutions) to declare legislation invalid, whereas no English court has that power. The fundamental principles of the common law can be applied to administrative action, and they can be applied as rules of interpretation—Cap. 29 has been quoted in such cases in the present century—to Acts of Parliament or statutory instruments, on the ground that 'Parliament could not have intended' that an interpretation contrary to fundamental principles be observed. The technique is illustrated by the famous dissenting judgments in *Rex v. Halliday* (1917) and *Liversidge v. Anderson* (1942). In both cases the majority of the Lords of Appeal accepted as valid statutory instruments which would have been declared invalid if there had not been a war raging. In both cases the dissenting Lords protested vehemently. Lord Atkin's words in the later case may perhaps be quoted:

> I view with apprehension the attitude of judges who on a mere question of construction [i.e. of an Act of Parliament] when face to face with claims involving the liberty of the subject show themselves more executive minded than the executive. In this country, amid the clash of arms, the laws are not silent. They may be changed, but they speak the same language in war as in peace. It has always been one of the pillars of freedom, one of the principles of liberty for which on recent authority [Sir Winston Churchill] we are now fighting, that the judges are no respecters of persons and stand between the subject and

any attempted encroachments on his liberty by the executive, alert to see that any coercive action is justified in law. In this case I have listened to arguments which might have been addressed acceptably to the Court of King's Bench in the time of Charles I. I protest, even if I do it alone, against a strained construction put on words with the effect of giving an uncontrolled power of imprisonment to the Minister.

Even Lord Atkin would have admitted, however, that if the Act of Parliament had been clearly expressed, the courts would have had to give effect to it, whereas in the United States the courts control legislation where they consider it outside the limits of constitutional powers.

The French Declarations of the Rights of Man had no such purpose. They were not founded on the existing law, as the American Bills of Rights were. They derived from the philosophers of the eighteenth century, who were to some extent influenced by Locke and British experience. There is, for instance, an echo of Cap. 29 of Magna Carta in article 7 of the Declaration of 1789.

No man should be accused, arrested, or imprisoned except in cases determined by the law, and according to the forms which it has prescribed. . . .

The purpose of declarations of this kind is not to have legislation declared invalid but to prescribe rules for the legislators to follow. Their efficiency therefore depends on the extent to which the principles enunciated are carried out in detail by legislation. To some extent this is true everywhere. Chapter 29 of Magna Carta is in itself of no great value. It is important only because its principles have been worked out by legislation and common law. Liberty of the person is secured not by a declaration of right but by adequate remedies before impartial tribunals whose decisions are respected and enforced. In the Commonwealth overseas, the United States, and some other countries, however, the Bills of Rights also imply judicial review of legislation. If it is desired that judicial review be excluded, provision is so made, as with the 'directive principles of State policy' in the Indian Constitution.

The people of Great Britain and of some of the older countries of the Commonwealth have been content to rely on the force of public opinion, the traditions of the Houses of Parliament, and the emphatic reiteration by judges and lawyers of the principles upon which the laws of England have been built up. Even in Canada, Australia and Northern Ireland, however, there are constitutional restrictions on legislation, as there are in Ceylon. In 1960 the Canadian Parliament decided to enact a declaratory Bill of Rights which can be used in the interpretation of federal legislation. It begins with Cap. 29 of Magna Carta:

> It is hereby recognized and declared that in Canada there have always existed and shall continue to exist without discrimination by reason of race, national origin, religion or sex the following human rights and fundamental freedoms, namely, the right of the individual to life, liberty, security of the person and enjoyment of property, and the right not to be deprived thereof except by due process of law.

In most of the newer countries of the Commonwealth there are formal Bills of Rights. One of the main reasons was the existence of differences of race, religion, language, caste or tribe which led to fears of discrimination. Mere non-discrimination clauses, as in Ireland in 1920, India in 1935, and Ceylon in 1946, were thought to be insufficient. What is more, the political leaders in Asia and Africa to whom power was transferred in and after 1947 believed firmly that their countries needed rapid social and economic development within a constitutional framework which protected the life, liberty and dignity of the ordinary citizen. Though often critical of British policy, many of them were graduates of British or American universities, or of universities of the British type in their own countries, and were anxious to establish, maintain and often to improve, the fundamental liberties which they had inherited with English law.

The precedent was set in Burma, whose Constitution of 1947 repeated the substance of Cap. 29 of Magna Carta, among other provisions, in the form, 'No citizen shall be deprived of his personal liberty, nor his dwelling entered, nor his property confiscated, save in accordance with law'. The Indian Constitution of 1950 has a much more elaborate Bill of Rights, in which Cap. 29 of Magna Carta is represented by article 21, 'No person shall be deprived of his life or personal liberty except according to procedure established by law'. The Indian Bill of Rights was adapted with many amendments in the Pakistan Constitution of 1956 and the Malayan Constitution of 1958, which became the Malaysian Constitution of 1963.

A new element in the situation was introduced by the Rome Convention of 1950, the European Convention for the Protection of Human Rights and Fundamental Freedoms. This was ratified by the United Kingdom in March 1951, and it came into force in September 1953. In 1953, too, the United Kingdom extended the Convention to all territories for whose international relations the government of the United Kingdom was responsible. The list of territories included all those which have become independent countries in the Commonwealth since 1953. No legislation was enacted, because it was thought that the fundamental liberties protected by the Convention were already protected by the laws, both in the United Kingdom and in the territories beyond the seas.

One effect of this development was, however, that the Bills of Rights of the newly independent countries in the West Indies and Africa were based on the Rome Convention. For instance, Cap. 29 of Magna Carta was replaced by a provision to the effect that no person should be deprived of his personal liberty save in certain cases and in accordance with a procedure permitted by law, and the cases were then specified and further detail relating to lawful imprisonment was set out.

The Bill of Rights in the Indian Constitution has been a considerable success because, though it has been lawfully amended, the Supreme Court and the High Courts of India have been able, in a series of valuable decisions, to work out the consequences in the light of the social and economic conditions of India. It must be said, however, that this is a consequence of the wise restraint of the leaders of the Congress party. The Bills of Rights throughout the Commonwealth, excepting only the Canadian Bills of Rights, are 'entrenched', in the sense that they cannot be amended by ordinary legislation. Entrenchment assumes, however, that there will always be a substantial minority on any question, whose assent will have to be secured. Experience has shown that this condition is not necessarily satisfied. The leaders who achieve independence, and the parties which they lead, secure such predominance that they find the enactment of constitutional amendments to be as easy as the enactment of the traditional Dogs Act.

VI Magna Carta and the future

THE CELEBRATION OF AN ANNIVERSARY, whether of a person, an institution or an event, tends towards exaggeration of his or its importance. The parliament summoned by Simon de Montfort, Earl of Leicester, in 1265 was significant in that it may have been the first occasion on which representatives of towns and cities were summoned. But the development of parliamentary institutions was continuous from the middle of the thirteenth century to the Revolution of 1688 and even to the present day. The issue of King John's Charter of 1215 was an event of great contemporary importance, and that Charter may be regarded as the prototype or first draft of the Charter which has retained permanent influence, the Magna Carta of 1225. It would not have been quoted so frequently if it had not contained Cap. 29, and most of Magna Carta is irrelevant to modern conditions. All four of the Charters would, however, have an honoured place in constitutional history, even without Cap. 29 or 39, because of the implication that even the king was under the law.

The influence of Magna Carta on the law of England has become so suffused that, apart from Cap. 29, it is seldom recognized. Indeed, the connection with Cap. 29 is not always noticed. There is a vast case law on the compulsory acquisition of property, whose essential idea derives from Cap. 29; but the decisions of the House of Lords, not Cap. 29, are considered to provide the legal foundations. Even in respect of personal liberty, Cap. 29 is only the moon in the great constellation of the common law.

In the other common law jurisdictions it is not even a moon. Where personal liberty is protected by a Bill of Rights, attention is necessarily directed towards the Bill, and the fact that one or two provisions derive from Magna Carta is interesting but irrelevant. It is even possible to exaggerate the importance of the connection between modern constitutionalism and Magna Carta. That there is such a connection cannot be doubted. What is more, the fact that appeal could be made to Magna Carta in the seventeenth century was of some help in keeping England on the constitutional path. On the other hand, the historians would probably insist that it was a minor element in a complicated historical evolution.

One important element in that evolution was that the House of Commons generally supported the common law against the Stuart Kings. Francis Bacon, in his argument in *Chudleigh's Case*, which was known as the Case of Perpetuities, which ran on from 1589 to 1595, expressed some apprehension that an Act of Parliament might sweep away what he called 'all these perpetuities', by which he meant especially the laws and liberties of England. In fact, no Act has done so; but the fact that it might be done led the revolted American colonies to establish legislatures with limited powers and to insert Bills of Rights into their written Constitutions. The example has been widely followed, though not all constitutions vest in the judges the responsibility for declaring legislation to be beyond the legislature's constitutional powers. Where 'judicial review' does exist in the United States and the Commonwealth it is particularly effective because the Constitution and the common law speak the same language and in large measure have a common content. This is noticeable in India as well as in the United States, because the Indian Codes are in large measure formulations of the common law.

The experience of some countries which became independent in and after 1947 has not always been happy, and there is a tendency both to challenge the doctrine of the separation of powers by giving predominance to one party and to infringe the essential principles to which centuries of experience have led the British peoples to adhere. In celebrating the 750th anniversary of King John's Charter of 1215, commonly called the first Magna Carta, and the 700th anniversary of Simon de Montfort's parliament of 1265, we do well to remind ourselves that most of the mistakes in the practice of government which could be made have at some time or other been committed in England or the United Kingdom.

The text of Magna Carta 1215

This translation by G. R. C. Davis, D Phil, F R Hist S, is reproduced by permission of the Trustees of the British Museum with certain minor alterations by Sir Ivor Jennings. It sets out to convey the sense rather than the precise wording of the original Latin.

Clauses marked (†) are still valid under the Charter of 1225, but with a few minor amendments. Clauses marked (*) were omitted in all later reissues of the charter. In the charter itself the clauses are not numbered, and the text reads continuously.

JOHN, by the grace of God King of England, Lord of Ireland, Duke of Normandy and Aquitaine, and Count of Anjou, to his archbishops, bishops, abbots, earls, barons, justices, foresters, sheriffs, stewards, servants, and to all his officials and loyal subjects, Greeting.

KNOW THAT BEFORE GOD, for the health of our soul and those of our ancestors and heirs, to the honour of God, the exaltation of the holy Church, and the better ordering of our kingdom, at the advice of our reverend fathers Stephen, archbishop of Canterbury, primate of all England, and cardinal of the holy Roman Church, Henry archbishop of Dublin, William bishop of London, Peter bishop of Winchester, Jocelin bishop of Bath and Glastonbury, Hugh bishop of Lincoln, Walter bishop of Coventry, Benedict bishop of Rochester, Master Pandulf subdeacon and member of the papal household, Brother Aymeric master of the knighthood of the Temple in England, William Marshal earl of Pembroke, William earl of Salisbury, William earl of Warren, William earl of Arundel, Alan de Galloway constable of Scotland, Warin Fitz Gerald, Peter Fitz Herbert, Hubert de Burgh seneschal of Poitou, Hugh de Neville, Matthew Fitz Herbert, Thomas Basset, Alan Basset, Philip Daubeny, Robert de Roppeley, John Marshal, John Fitz Hugh, and other loyal subjects:

†(1) FIRST, THAT WE HAVE GRANTED TO GOD, and by this present charter have confirmed for us and our heirs in perpetuity, that the English Church shall be free, and shall have its rights undiminished, and its liberties unimpaired.

That we wish this so to be observed, appears from the fact that of our own free will, before the outbreak of the present dispute between us and our barons, we granted and confirmed by charter the freedom of the Church's elections—a right reckoned to be of the greatest necessity and importance to it—and caused this to be confirmed by Pope Innocent III. This freedom we shall observe ourselves, and desire to be observed in good faith by our heirs in perpetuity.

TO ALL FREE MEN OF OUR KINGDOM we have also granted, for us and our heirs for ever, all the liberties written out below, to have and to keep for them and their heirs, of us and our heirs:

(2) If any earl, baron, or other person that holds lands directly of the Crown, for military service, shall die, and at his death his heir shall be of full age and owe a 'relief', the heir shall have his inheritance on payment of the ancient scale of 'relief'. That is to say, the heir or heirs of an earl shall pay £100 for the entire earl's barony, the heir or heirs of a knight 100s. at most for the entire knight's 'fee', and any man that owes less shall pay less, in accordance with the ancient usage of 'fees'.

(3) But if the heir of such a person is under age and a ward, when he comes of age he shall have his inheritance without 'relief' or fine.

(4) The guardian of the land of an heir who is under age shall take from it only reasonable revenues, customary dues, and feudal services. He shall do this without destruction or damage to men or property. If we have given the guardianship of the land to a sheriff, or to any person answerable to us for the revenues, and he commits destruction or damage, we will exact compensation from him, and the land shall be entrusted to two worthy and prudent men of the same 'fee', who shall be answerable to us for the revenues, or to the person to whom we have assigned them. If we have given or sold to anyone the guardianship of such land, and he causes destruction or damage, he shall lose the guardianship of it, and it shall be handed over to two worthy and prudent men of the same 'fee', who shall be similarly answerable to us.

(5) For so long as a guardian has guardianship of such land, he shall maintain the houses, parks, fish preserves, ponds, mills, and everything else pertaining to it, from the revenues of the land itself. When the heir comes of age, he shall restore the whole land to him, stocked with plough teams and such implements of husbandry as the season demands and the revenues from the land can reasonably bear.

(6) Heirs may be given in marriage, but not to someone of lower social standing. Before a marriage takes place, it shall be made known to the heir's next-of-kin.

(7) At her husband's death, a widow may have her marriage portion and inheritance at once and without trouble. She shall pay nothing for her dower, marriage portion, or any inheritance that she and her husband held jointly on the day of his death. She may remain in her husband's house for forty days after his death, and within this period her dower shall be assigned to her.

(8) No widow shall be compelled to marry, so long as she wishes to remain without a husband. But she must give security that she will not marry without royal consent, if she holds her lands of the Crown, or without the consent of whatever other lord she may hold them of.

†(9) Neither we nor our officials will seize any land or rent in payment of a debt, so long as the debtor has movable goods sufficient to discharge the debt. A debtor's sureties shall not be dis-

trained upon so long as the debtor himself can discharge his debt. If, for lack of means, the debtor is unable to discharge his debt, his sureties shall be answerable for it. If they so desire, they may have the debtor's lands and rents until they have received satisfaction for the debt that they paid for him, unless the debtor can show that he has settled his obligations to them.

*(10) If anyone who has borrowed a sum of money from Jews dies before the debt has been repaid, his heir shall pay no interest on the debt for so long as he remains under age, irrespective of whom he holds his lands. If such a debt falls into the hands of the Crown, it will take nothing except the principal sum specified in the bond.

*(11) If a man dies owing money to Jews, his wife may have her dower and pay nothing towards the debt from it. If he leaves children that are under age, their needs may also be provided for on a scale appropriate to the size of his holding of lands. The debt is to be paid out of the residue, reserving the service due to his feudal lords. Debts owed to persons other than Jews are to be dealt with similarly.

*(12) No 'scutage' or 'aid' may be levied in our kingdom without general consent, unless it is for the ransom of our person, to make our eldest son a knight, and (once) to marry our eldest daughter. For these purposes only a reasonable 'aid' may be levied. 'Aids' from the city of London are to be treated similarly.

†(13) The city of London shall enjoy all its ancient liberties and free customs, both by land and by water. We also will and grant that all other cities, boroughs, towns, and ports shall enjoy all their liberties and free customs.

*(14) To obtain the general consent for the assessment of an 'aid'—except in the three cases specified above—or a 'scutage', we will cause the archbishops, bishops, abbots, earls, and greater barons to be summoned individually by letter. To those who hold lands directly of us we will cause a general summons to be issued, through the sheriffs and other officials, to come together on a fixed day (of which at least forty days notice shall be given) and at a fixed place. In all letters of summons, the cause of the summons will be stated. When a summons has been issued, the business appointed for the day shall go forward in accordance with the resolution of those present, even if not all those who were summoned have appeared.

*(15) In future we will allow no one to levy an 'aid' from his free men, except to ransom his person, to make his eldest son a knight, and (once) to marry his eldest daughter. For these purposes only a reasonable 'aid' may be levied.

(16) No man shall be forced to perform more service for a knight's 'fee', or other free holding of land, than is due from it.

(17) Ordinary lawsuits shall not follow the royal court around, but shall be held in a fixed place.

(18) Inquests of *novel disseisin, mort d'ancestor,* and *darrein presentment* shall be taken only in their proper county court. We ourselves, or in our absence abroad our chief justice, will send two justices to each county four times a year, and these justices, with four knights of the county elected by the county itself, shall hold the assizes in the county court, on the day and in the place where the court meets.

(19) If any assizes cannot be taken on the day of the county court, as many knights and freeholders shall afterwards remain behind, of those who have attended the court, as will suffice for the administration of justice, having regard to the volume of business to be done.

†(20) For a trivial offence, a free man shall be fined only in proportion to the degree of his offence, and for a serious offence correspondingly, but not so heavily as to deprive him of his livelihood. In the same way, a merchant shall be spared his merchandise, and a husbandman the implements of his husbandry, if they fall upon the mercy of a royal court. None of these fines shall be imposed except by the assessment of reputable men of the neighbourhood.

†(21) Earls and barons shall be fined only by their equals, and in proportion to the gravity of their offence.

†(22) A fine imposed upon the lay property of a clerk in holy orders shall be assessed upon the same principles, without reference to the value of his ecclesiastical benefice.

†(23) No town or person shall be forced to build bridges over rivers except those with an ancient obligation to do so.

(24) No sheriff, constable, coroners, or other royal officials are to hold lawsuits that should be held by the royal justices.

*(25) Every county, hundred, wapentake, and tithing shall remain at its ancient rent, without increase, except the royal demesne manors.

(26) If at the death of a man who holds a lay 'fee' of the Crown, a sheriff or royal official produces royal letters patent of summons for a debt due to the Crown, it shall be lawful for them to seize and list movable goods found in the lay 'fee' of the dead man to the value of the debt, as assessed by worthy men. Nothing shall be removed until the whole debt is paid, when the residue shall be given over to the executors to carry out the dead man's will. If no debt is due to the Crown, all the movable goods shall be regarded as the property of the dead man, except the reasonable shares of his wife and children.

*(27) If a free man dies intestate, his movable goods are to be distributed by his next-of-kin and friends, under the supervision of the Church. The rights of his debtors are to be preserved.

(28) No constable or other royal official shall take corn or other movable goods from any man without immediate payment, unless the seller voluntarily offers postponement of this.

(29) No constable may compel a knight to pay money for castle-guard if the knight is willing to undertake the guard in person, or with reasonable excuse to supply some other fit man to do it. A knight taken or sent on military service shall be excused from castle-guard for the period of this service.

(30) No sheriff, royal official, or other person shall take horses or carts for transport from any free man, without his consent.

(31) Neither we nor any royal official will take wood for our castle, or for any other purpose, without the consent of the owner.

(32) We will not keep the lands of people convicted of felony in our hand for longer than a year and a day, after which they shall be returned to the lords of the 'fees' concerned.

†(33) All fish-weirs shall be removed from the Thames, the Medway, and

throughout the whole of England, except on the sea coast.

(34) The writ called *precipe* shall not in future be issued to anyone in respect of any holding of land, if a free man could thereby be deprived of the right of trial in his own lord's court.

(35) There shall be standard measures of wine, ale, and corn (the London quarter), throughout the kingdom. There shall also be a standard width of dyed cloth, russett, and haberject, namely two ells within the selvedges. Weights are to be standardised similarly.

(36) In future nothing shall be paid or accepted for the issue of a writ of inquisition of life or limbs. It shall be given *gratis*, and not refused.

(37) If a man holds land of the Crown by 'fee-farm', 'socage', or 'burgage', and also holds land of someone else for knight's service, we will not have guardianship of his heir, nor of the land that belongs to the other person's 'fee', by virtue of the 'fee-farm', 'socage', or 'burgage', unless the 'fee-farm' owes knight's service. We will not have the guardianship of a man's heir, or of land that he holds of someone else, by reason of any small property that he may hold of the Crown for a service of knives, arrows, or the like.

(38) In future no official shall place a man on trial upon his own unsupported statement, without producing credible witnesses to the truth of it.

†(39) No free man shall be seized or imprisoned, or stripped of his rights or possessions, or outlawed or exiled, or deprived of his standing in any other way, nor will we proceed with force against him, or send others to do so, except by the lawful judgement of his equals or by the law of the land.

†(40) To no one will we sell, to no one deny or delay right or justice.

†(41) All merchants may enter or leave England unharmed and without fear, and may stay or travel within it, by land or water, for purposes of trade, free from all illegal exactions, in accordance with ancient and lawful customs. This, however, does not apply in time of war to merchants from a country that is at war with us. Any such merchants found in our country at the outbreak of war shall be detained without injury to their persons or property, until we or our chief

justice have discovered how our own merchants are being treated in the country at war with us. If our own merchants are safe they shall be safe too.

*(42) In future it shall be lawful for any man to leave and return to our kingdom unharmed and without fear, by land or water, preserving his allegiance to us, except in time of war, for some short period, for the common benefit of the realm. People that have been imprisoned or outlawed in accordance with the law of the land, people from a country that is at war with us, and merchants—who shall be dealt with as stated above—are excepted from this provision.

(43) If a man holds lands of any 'escheat' such as the 'honour' of Wallingford, Nottingham, Boulogne, Lancaster or of other 'escheats' in our hand that are baronies, at his death his heir shall give us only the 'relief' and service that he would have made to the baron, had the barony been in the baron's hand. We will hold the 'escheat' in the same manner as the baron held it.

†(44) People who live outside the forest need not in future appear before the royal justices of the forest in answer to general summonses, unless they are actually involved in proceedings or are sureties for someone who has been seized for a forest offence.

*(45) We will appoint as justices, constables, sheriffs, or other officials, only men that know the law of the realm and are minded to keep it well.

(46) All barons who have founded abbeys, and have charters of English kings or ancient tenure as evidence of this, may have guardianship of them when there is no abbot, as is their due.

(47) †All forests that have been created in our reign shall at once be disafforested.† River-banks that have been enclosed in our reign shall be treated similarly.

*(48) All evil customs relating to forests and warrens, foresters, warreners, sheriffs and their servants, or river-banks and their wardens, are at once to be investigated in every county by twelve sworn knights of the county, and within forty days of their enquiry the evil customs are to be abolished completely and irrevocably. But we, or our chief justice if we are not in England, are first to be informed.

*(49) We will at once return all hostages and charters delivered up to us by

Englishmen as security for peace or for loyal service.

*(50) We will remove completely from their offices the kinsmen of Gerard de Athée, and in future they shall hold no offices in England. The people in question are Engelard de Cigogné, Peter Guy, and Andrew de Chanceaux, Guy de Cigogné, Geoffrey de Martigny and his brothers, Philip Marc and his brothers, with Geoffrey his nephew, and all their followers.

*(51) As soon as peace is restored, we will remove from the kingdom all the foreign knights, bowmen, their attendants, and the mercenaries that have come to it, to its harm, with horses and arms.

*(52) To any man whom we have deprived or dispossessed of lands, castles, liberties, or rights, without the lawful judgement of his equals, we will at once restore these. In cases of dispute the matter shall be resolved by the judgement of the twenty-five barons referred to below in the clause for securing the peace (§ 61). In cases, however, where a man was deprived or dispossessed of something without the lawful judgement of his equals by our father King Henry or our brother King Richard, and it remains in our hands or is held by others under our warranty, we shall have respite for the period commonly allowed to Crusaders, unless a lawsuit had been begun, or an enquiry had been made at our order, before we took the Cross as a Crusader. On our return from the Crusade, or if we abandon it, we will at once render justice in full.

*(53) We shall have similar respite in rendering justice in connexion with forests that are to be disafforested, or to remain forests, when these were first afforested by our father Henry or our brother Richard; with the guardianship of lands in another person's 'fee', when we have hitherto had this by virtue of a 'fee' held of us for knight's service by a third party; and with abbeys founded in another person's 'fee', in which the lord of the 'fee' claims to own a right. On our return from the Crusade, or if we abandon it, we will at once do full justice to complaints about these matters.

(54) No one shall be arrested or imprisoned on the appeal of a woman for the death of any person except her husband.

*(55) All fines that have been given to us unjustly and against the law of the land, and all fines that we have exacted un-

justly, shall be entirely remitted or the matter decided by a majority judgement of the twenty-five barons referred to below in the clause for securing the peace (§ 61) together with Stephen, archbishop of Canterbury, if he can be present, and such others as he wishes to bring with him. If the archbishop cannot be present, proceedings shall continue without him, provided that if any of the twenty-five barons has been involved in a similar suit himself, his judgement shall be set aside, and someone else chosen and sworn in his place, as a substitute for the single occasion, by the rest of the twenty-five.

(56) If we have deprived or dispossessed any Welshmen of lands, liberties, or anything else in England or in Wales, without the lawful judgement of their equals, these are at once to be returned to them. A dispute on this point shall be determined in the Marches by the judgement of equals. English law shall apply to holdings of land in England, Welsh law to those in Wales, and the law of the Marches to those in the Marches. The Welsh shall treat us and ours in the same way.

*(57) In cases where a Welshman was deprived or dispossessed of anything, without the lawful judgement of his equals, by our father King Henry or our brother King Richard, and it remains in our hands or is held by others under our warranty, we shall have respite for the period commonly allowed to Crusaders, unless a lawsuit had been begun, or an enquiry had been made at our order, before we took the Cross as a Crusader. But on our return from the Crusade, or if we abandon it, we will at once do full justice according to the laws of Wales and the said regions.

*(58) We will at once return the son of Llywelyn, all Welsh hostages, and the charters delivered to us as security for the peace.

*(59) With regard to the return of the sisters and hostages of Alexander, king of Scotland, his liberties and his rights, we will treat him in the same way as our other barons of England, unless it appears from the charters that we hold from his father William, formerly king of Scotland, that he should be treated otherwise. This matter shall be resolved by the judgement of his equals in our court.

(60) All these customs and liberties that we have granted shall be observed in our kingdom in so far as concerns our own relations with our subjects. Let all men of our kingdom, whether clergy or laymen, observe them similarly in their relations with their own men.

*(61) SINCE WE HAVE GRANTED ALL THESE THINGS for God, for the better ordering of our kingdom, and to allay the discord that has arisen between us and our barons, and since we desire that they shall be enjoyed in their entirety, with lasting strength, for ever, we give and grant to the barons the following security:

The barons shall elect twenty-five of their number to keep, and cause to be observed with all their might, the peace and liberties granted and confirmed to them by this charter.

If we, our chief justice, our officials, or any of our servants offend in any respect against any man, or transgress any of the articles of the peace or of this security, and the offence is made known to four of the said twenty-five barons, they shall come to us—or in our absence from the kingdom to the chief justice—to declare it and claim immediate redress. If we, or in our absence abroad the chief justice, make no redress within forty days, reckoning from the day on which the offence was declared to us or to him, the four barons shall refer the matter to the rest of the twenty-five barons, who may distrain upon and assail us in every way possible, with the support of the whole community of the land, by seizing our castles, lands, possessions, or anything else saving only our own person and those of the queen and our children, until they have secured such redress as they have determined upon. Having secured the redress, they may then resume their normal obedience to us.

Any man who so desires may take an oath to obey the commands of the twenty-five barons for the achievement of these ends, and to join with them in assailing us to the utmost of his power. We give public and free permission to take this oath to any man who so desires, and at no time will we prohibit any man from taking it. Indeed, we will compel any of our subjects who are unwilling to take it to swear it at our command.

If one of the twenty-five barons dies or leaves the country, or is prevented in any other way from discharging his duties, the rest of them shall choose another baron in his place, at their discretion, who shall be duly sworn in as they were.

In the event of disagreement among the twenty-five barons on any matter referred to them for decision, the verdict of the majority present shall have the same validity as a unanimous verdict of the whole twenty-five, whether these were all present or some of those summoned were unwilling or unable to appear.

The twenty-five barons shall swear to obey all the above articles faithfully, and shall cause them to be obeyed by others to the best of their power.

We will not seek to procure from anyone, either by our own efforts or those of a third party, anything by which any part of these concessions or liberties might be revoked or diminished. Should such a thing be procured, it shall be null and void and we will at no time make use of it, either ourselves or through a third party.

*(62) We have remitted and pardoned fully to all men any ill-will, hurt, or grudges that have arisen between us and our subjects, whether clergy or laymen, since the beginning of the dispute. We have in addition remitted fully, and for our own part have also pardoned, to all clergy and laymen any offences committed as a result of the said dispute between Easter in the sixteenth year of our reign (i.e. 1215) and the restoration of peace.

In addition we have caused letters patent to be made for the barons, bearing witness to this security and to the concessions set out above, over the seals of Stephen archbishop of Canterbury, Henry archbishop of Dublin, the other bishops named above, and Master Pandulf.

*(63) IT IS ACCORDINGLY OUR WISH AND COMMAND that the English Church shall be free, and that men in our kingdom shall have and keep all these liberties, rights, and concessions, well and peaceably in their fulness and entirety for them and their heirs, of us and our heirs, in all things and all places for ever.

Both we and the barons have sworn that all this shall be observed in good faith and without deceit. Witness the abovementioned people and many others.

Given by our hand in the meadow that is called Runnymede, between Windsor and Staines, on the fifteenth day of June in the seventeenth year of our reign (i.e. 1215: *the new regnal year began on 28 May*).

Printed in England for Her Majesty's Stationery Office by Trade Union Labor by Headley Brothers Ltd London and Ashford Kent